BETTER HEALTH:

IMPROVING HEALTH PROMOTION AND HEALTH CARE FOR PEOPLE WITH A LEARNING DISABILITY

Unit 3
Treatment

First Draft Publications

Series Editor: John Harris

Published by
bild

Wolverhampton Road, Kidderminster
Worcestershire DY10 3PP

ISBN 1 902519 25 6

Acknowledgements

BILD would like to thank everyone who assisted in the development of these materials and, in particular, colleagues who commented on various drafts. Special thanks to Lesley Barcham, Sue Bikerton, John Brooke, Paul Eggett, Gill Levy, Phil Madden and Chris Sturdy.

The development and publication of these materials was made possible by a grant from the Department of Health.

BETTER HEALTH:

IMPROVING HEALTH PROMOTION AND HEALTH CARE FOR PEOPLE WITH A LEARNING DISABILITY

Unit 3

Treatment

Prepared for BILD by
John Harris, Neill Simpson
and Jackie Rodgers

BETTER HEALTH:

IMPROVING HEALTH PROMOTION AND HEALTH CARE FOR PEOPLE WITH A LEARNING DISABILITY

If you wish to use these independent study units to support BILD Distance Learning, you must first register with the BILD Distance Learning Programme. Please contact the BILD Distance Learning Co-ordinator at BILD, Wolverhampton Road, Kidderminster, DY10 3PP.

If you wish to use these materials to work towards a BILD Certificate in Learning Disability Studies, you must be registered on a BILD validated course. To find out if your course has been validated by BILD, speak to the course tutor, or contact the BILD Validation Office, at BILD, Wolverhampton Road, Kidderminster, DY10 3PP.

Unit 3

CONTENTS

Unit 3

Introduction

This unit looks at what happens when someone with a learning disability needs medical treatment. The term 'treatment' is used to describe any form of intervention which is intended to improve the outcome of illness or improve a person's health. This includes:

- relieving symptoms
- reducing disability
- improving the quality of life.

Treatments can take many forms, some of which are described in this unit. Most treatments will be arranged and supervised by a healthcare professional. However, to be effective, treatments often require the participation and co-operation of the person who is ill. Without help and support, many people with a learning disability find it difficult to participate in treatment. As a result, they may be ill for longer and suffer more from poor health than other members of the community.

Staff and other carers can play an important part in making sure that people with a learning disability gain maximum benefit from the many different forms of treatment which are available.

Unit 3

1 Learning outcomes

At the end of this unit you will be able to:

- Describe what is meant by 'treatment'.
- Describe different ways of supporting people receiving routine medical treatments such as an injection.
- Explain the kind of support which might be helpful to people before, during and after admission to hospital.
- Explain what is involved in giving consent to treatment.
- Suggest how you can help people with a learning disability give consent and what options are available if they cannot give consent.
- Explain what is meant by 'chronic' and 'terminal' illness and how to support people with a learning disability with a chronic or terminal illness.
- Explain why people with a learning disability may have difficulty in understanding what happens when someone dies.
- Describe typical responses to bereavement and how to help.
- Describe the support which may be helpful to anyone who is dying.

  There are 7 activities in this unit.

2 What do we mean by treatment ?

Activity 1
Which of the following are examples of treatment which might be recommended by a GP?

1. You are still in pain after falling down the stairs. Take two aspirin tablets after meals.
2. Your arthritis is getting worse. Go to the physiotherapist twice a week for the next six weeks.
3. You have a weak heart. Stop smoking and don't drink more than two glasses of wine a day.
4. Change this dressing twice a day and use this antiseptic ointment.
5. You have to go into hospital to have your wisdom tooth removed.
6. You are very overweight. Reduce your weight by at least 10 lbs.
7. You have a nasty chest infection. Take this prescription to the chemist and take three tablets a day until the bottle is empty.
8. I'm giving you an anti-tetanus injection in case the cut on your hand has been infected.
9. You have to go to hospital to have the broken bone in your foot put in plaster.
10. Your eyesight is very bad. I think you will need glasses.

Comment
All these interventions are examples of 'treatment' which could be recommended by a GP. They are all designed to overcome illness or some of the causes of poor health.

Treatment might be given as a 'one off' event at the doctor's surgery or it might involve a series of visits to the hospital as an 'outpatient'. For people who are seriously ill, or where the treatment itself presents significant risks, it might involve admission to hospital. In all these situations, the person with a learning disability is likely to need preparation before the visit, support during the visit and continuing advice and encouragement afterwards.

This course is not intended to provide you with specialised medical knowledge or to enable you to decide what treatment is or is not desirable. This is the responsibility of the health care professionals including the GP and doctors and nurses working in hospitals. This unit explains how a non-medical member of staff can help people with a learning disability to make good use of the health service when they need treatment. It covers:

- preparation for treatment;
- support during treatment;
- continuing care after treatment;
- consent to treatment;
- long term support for people with chronic illness;
- support for people who are bereaved;
- preparation for dying.

By working closely with health care professionals you can make sure that people with a learning disability get high quality care which is appropriate to their needs.

2.2 Alternatives to conventional treatments

This course is primarily concerned with health care which is available through the National Health Service and, to this extent, it focuses on traditional or mainstream forms of medical treatment. However, it is important to recognise that many non-disabled people place great reliance upon alternative or complementary therapies and there may be occasions when these different approaches to treatment can also be helpful to people with a learning disability. The main types of alternative medicine are:

Homeopathy – using 'natural' or herbal ingredients to make 'medicine'

Acupuncture – based on the Chinese practice of inserting thin needles into the body to alleviate pain

Chiropractic – the manipulation of the spine

Osteopathy – the manipulation of different bones and joints

Aromatherapy – the use of 'smell' and aromatic oils to increase physical and mental health.

These approaches can be grouped together because they all fall outside the range of treatments which are usually available on the National Health. In most cases, the person receiving the treatment has to pay the therapist. Apart from this, all the 'complementary' therapies are very different from each other.

The fact that these therapies are not usually available as part of the NHS does not mean that they are ineffective. Many substances used in conventional medicine were originally herbal remedies. Foxglove (digitalis) is a good example of a very powerful naturally occurring drug which is now used to treat illness. Similarly, evening primrose oil has become more widely used and its active ingredient has been licensed for use as a prescription medicine. Some of the 'remedies' produced from naturally occurring ingredients by homeopaths are extremely potent and, if misused, they could be dangerous.

Although there is a tendency to view complementary therapies as 'natural', this does not mean that they are harmless. For example, evening primrose oil can increase the likelihood of a person with epilepsy having a fit. In addition, complementary remedies may interact with conventional treatments causing unexpected consequences. It is therefore important that the GP is always told about any complementary (natural or herbal) remedies that are being used. Anyone seeking information about any form of alternative or complementary therapy should contact an experienced practitioner who is accredited by an established professional body.

New therapies, which are shown to be both safe and effective, are likely to be accepted as mainstream medicine. However, overall there is little scientific evidence regarding the effect of these alternatives to mainstream medicine and for this reason we would recommend that they are treated with great caution.

The rest of this unit looks at the different kinds of treatment which are available on the NHS and how you can help people with a learning disability to make good use of them. The next section considers treatment which requires a low level of medical input and can therefore be carried out in the doctor's surgery or at an out-patient clinic attached to a hospital.

3 Treatments requiring general medical services

Treatments which are quick and easy to administer are very often available as soon as the doctor has made a diagnosis (see Unit 1). While this is very convenient, it means that there is often very little time to prepare the person with a learning disability. While some people may benefit from not having had any time to worry and become anxious about treatment, others will need time to make the transition from ‘finding out what’s wrong’ to ‘treatment to make you better’.

Of course, if the treatment is simple and involves no discomfort, this may not matter. However, if it involves an injection or the application of medicines in sensitive areas (for example, suppositories or eye-drops) the person with a learning disability may wish to take a little time to prepare for the treatment. In this situation, staff who are supporting the person with a learning disability can help by:

- explaining to the person what kind of treatment is being proposed;
- making it clear to the person that they have a choice about when the treatment is given;
- discussing the benefits and disadvantages for that person of being treated straightaway or waiting.

In the next few pages we consider some of the main types of treatment and how staff and carers can provide support.

3.2 Injections

Many people are scared of needles and, in particular, associate injections with pain. This may be because of past experience or because of exaggerated accounts of painful injections given by other people. People with a learning disability experience pain in the same way as anyone else, and there is no justification for believing that people with more severe disability are less sensitive to pain. However, the experience of pain is made worse by anxiety, depression, or feeling that you have no control over what is happening to you. For this reason, it may be better to postpone injections for people who express high levels of anxiety until they have been given appropriate preparation.

Unit 3

Preparation for injections

There are three important things that you can do to help someone with a learning disability prepare for an injection.

- First, tell them what is going to happen, where they will have the injection and, as far as possible explain what it might feel like. For example, an injection in the skin 'feels like someone pinching you with their finger tips' while a muscle injection feels more like 'the bruise you would feel after being punched or poked'. Make it clear that it only hurts for a very short time.

- Second, try to get the person to take responsibility for having the injection. In other words, explain why, for the good of their health, they should have the injection. As mentioned above, everyone copes with pain and discomfort more effectively if they feel they have control in the situation.

- Third, suggest some simple strategies which can help while the injection is being given and if necessary, practise these before-hand:

  look away – seeing a needle puncture our skin leads us to anticipate pain and focus on the sensation of pain;

  try to relax – one way of doing this is to take long slow breaths;

  think about something unrelated to the injection, for example, a recent TV programme or what you will eat for dinner later in the day. Staff can help by encouraging the person to talk about some thing they enjoy. It is a good idea to prepare a list of things to talk about beforehand.

Sometimes you may be tempted to suggest a person with a learning disability has an injection without preparation. For example, someone who has never previously had an injection may not know what to expect and for this reason you might think they will be less anxious if they don't have any preparation. The danger of this approach is that the next time the person requires an injection they might be very apprehensive and you may find it hard to regain their trust.

3.3 Preparation for other medical procedures

Sometimes, after a visit to the GP, the patient will be asked to come back at a later date or to visit an out-patient clinic at a hospital to receive treatment. The more you know about what will happen and what procedures are involved in the treatment, the better you will be able to prepare the person with a learning disability. Here are some things you can do to find out:

- If you are with the person when they visit the GP, ask him or her what is involved in the treatment. Explain that you will be able to spend time passing on this information to the person with a learning disability.

- Ask if there is a practice nurse who could explain to you and the person with a learning disability what the treatment will involve.

- Ask if the GP or practice nurse could arrange for the person with a learning disability to visit the clinic in advance of the treatment so that they know what to expect.

- If you anticipate the treatment will cause pain or discomfort, follow the suggestions for preparing a person with a learning disability to have an injection.

- If the person you are supporting is likely to be distressed or anxious while waiting for treatment, contact the staff at the surgery or clinic in advance and ask them if it is possible for the person to be seen as soon as they arrive. It may be helpful to book the person in as the first or last appointment of the day. (See Unit 2 Section 4.5 for further suggestions on providing support when visiting the GP).

Activity 2

Read through the following story and make a note of anything Sally, the keyworker, does to help Gaynor prepare for having treatment.

Gaynor was aware of her tooth from the moment she woke up. To begin with there was just a dull ache, but during breakfast, while she was chewing her toast, it suddenly became very painful. Sally, her keyworker, arranged an emergency visit to the dentist later that day.

Unit 3

The dentist was very busy and only had time for a quick look inside Gaynor's mouth. When he touched her tooth she screamed and started crying.

The dentist said Gaynor would have to make an appointment to come back the following day so that he could 'fix her up'. As they were going out it occurred to Sally that she had better find out what the dentist meant by 'fixing'.

While Gaynor was putting on her coat, Sally asked the dentist what kind of treatment he was planning. 'Oh the tooth's beyond repair. The best thing to do is to whip it out.'

Sally asked what was involved. 'Oh just a local anaesthetic, a couple of quick injections that's all, and then we should be able to lift it out without any trouble'.

'I see' said Sally, thinking about the state that Gaynor might be in the following day. 'Anything we can do between now and then?'

'Not really' said the dentist, 'painkillers might help to numb the pain a bit, but don't let her have too many'.

'OK, thanks, see you tomorrow' said Sally, wondering how she could persuade Gaynor to come back the following day.

Sally stopped at the chemist to get some painkillers and when they got home she made Gaynor a warm drink and gave her the recommended dose. A bit later, after Gaynor had settled down and watched some TV programmes, Sally explained that she needed to go back to the dentist to have her tooth out. Gaynor wailed and said she didn't want to go.

What can Sally and her colleagues do now to help Gaynor prepare for having her tooth extracted?

Comment

In the story, Sally has arranged for Gaynor to visit the dentist to find out what treatment she needs. She has found out some useful information:

> Gaynor has been advised to have a tooth extracted;
>
> she will need a local anaesthetic;
>
> she can take some pain killers to numb the pain.

Other things that the staff can do to prepare Gaynor include:

- explaining what happens during a tooth extraction;
- explaining how the anaesthetic injection will help;
- describing what this might feel like and that it only lasts a very short period of time;
- finding someone else who has had a tooth taken out and can talk about it in a positive way;
- suggesting things Gaynor can do to relax at the dentist;
- helping Gaynor to practise some simple relaxation techniques;
- demonstrating a calm and relaxed approach to give Gaynor confidence.

Points for practice
Most people with a learning disability will benefit from preparation before they receive minor medical treatments such as an injection or a tooth extraction.

3.4 Support during medical procedures

Sending the right emotional signals
It is a natural human response to pick up emotional cues from other people and for these cues to influence our own feelings. For example, if everyone else is enjoying a party it's difficult not to join in and feel happy as well. In the same way, if we show by our behaviour that we are feeling anxious or fearful, other people close to us may notice and start to share our feelings. This is particularly likely to happen in strange surroundings, such as a hospital, where we are not sure what to expect.

The idea that we naturally communicate our feelings to other people has important implications for supporting people with a learning disability when they receive hospital treatment. It means that if you feel apprehensive, anxious or fearful, the person you are trying to support is also likely to feel the same way. On the other hand, if you are relaxed, confident and self-assured, the person you are with is more likely to be put at ease. If you are particularly sensitive about any aspect of medical treatments, for example the smell of hospitals or the sight of blood, you should think very carefully about whether or not you are the right person to offer support to a person with a learning disability in this sort of situation.

Providing information to the person with a learning disability

Medical treatment often involves a range of unusual experiences. Sometimes the medical staff take the trouble to explain what is happening, but it is not unusual for patients to be left uninformed about why they need to undress, what a particular procedure is designed to do or why they are left alone waiting. You can help the person with a learning disability by finding out as much as you can and then explaining to them in ways which they are most likely to understand. Here are some examples:

> A doctor provides an explanation of what is going to happen, but she speaks quickly and uses a number of long words. You can help by explaining what the doctor said using words, signs or pictures, which the person with a learning disability can understand. Take a pad and pencil along so that you can draw simple pictures or diagrams.
>
> Neither the doctors nor nurses offer an explanation about what is happening. You can help by asking them to tell you what the treatment involves, so that you can explain this for the person with a learning disability. Ask if they have a leaflet or, if not, ask if they can write down what will happen.
>
> No one has told you what to expect, and you have been left alone, waiting for something to happen. In this situation, you can only make a sensible guess about what is actually happening, but this can provide the person with a learning disability with a useful starting point for making sense of an otherwise confusing situation. For example, you might suggest any of the following:
>
> 'I expect we have to wait until the doctor has finished seeing another patient'

'I think they are waiting for the results of your X-ray to come back'

'You have to wait until the medicine they gave you starts to work'

'We've got to wait until a nurse comes to show us where to go next'

Providing information to the medical staff

In most settings, the medical staff will be keen to help the person with a learning disability and adjust their procedures to avoid distress or discomfort. However, they will probably have had little direct experience of people with a learning disability in general and they may know nothing about the particular person you are supporting. They will rely upon you to help them respond appropriately to the person you are with.

Here are some general suggestions:

- Do encourage the doctors and nurses to speak directly to the person with a learning disability. Even if the person has little or no spoken language, it is important that other people establish a relationship, through eye contact, facial expression, body language and verbal intonation.

- Explain your role in providing the person with information and reassurance.

- Don't be afraid of telling the medical staff if you know that the person you are with is likely to experience particular problems with any of the treatment procedures, for example, some people may only be able to take liquid medicines (not tablets). Others may be reluctant to undress in a strange place or to be seen by strange people without their clothes on. Tell staff what to do to get the person to co-operate.

- If the person presents any unusual or challenging behaviours, reassure the medical staff about what these behaviours mean and explain how they should respond, for example, 'Imran often claps his hands together when he meets new people. He'll settle down in a few minutes when you've said hello and he's got used to the sound of your voices'.

Points for practice
Provide support during minor treatments by explaining what is happening and helping the doctors and nurses to relate positively to the person with a learning disability.

Activity 3
From your own recent experience, think of one person you know well who has received treatment at the GP surgery or at an outpatient clinic. Use the headings provided to answer the following questions:

What support did the person receive?

How effective was this support?

What additional support could have been provided?

- Preparation
- Emotional support during treatment
- Explaining what is happening during treatment
- Helping medical staff to respond to the person

Comment
Did the support you and your colleagues provided cover all four headings? Looking back on the experience, there are probably things which you have learned about the person with a learning disability and about the health professionals who provided the treatment. Hopefully you can use this knowledge in the future.

3.5 Follow-up care and monitoring

After receiving treatment, there is often a period during which the patient needs to take special care. This might involve:

taking medicines on a regular basis;

adjusting routines and behaviour until the treatment has had an effect on the person's illness;

monitoring progress and speaking to the doctor if there is any adverse reaction or if the treatment does not seem to be working.

Many people with a learning disability will be able to take an active role in their own care after treatment. However, they will be better able to help themselves if staff take the time to explain exactly what they should or should not do and why this is necessary. People who need to do certain things on a regular basis (for example, taking medicines; doing exercises; providing urine samples) are likely to benefit from memory aids, for example a chart which reminds them when to exercise, or a picture of some tablets on their bedside table. Many pharmacies (chemist's shops which provide medicines on prescription) provide aids to help people take their medicines properly.

Even where you feel that staff should closely monitor follow-up care, for example, in the case of strong medicines, it is important that you help the person with a learning disability to take an active role, rather than making them the passive recipient of care which is provided by other people.

If you are involved in supporting a person with a learning disability for treatment as an out-patient at a doctor's surgery or a hospital, you may find the following publications useful: *Going to Outpatient's*, by Sheila Hollins, Jane Bernal and Matthew Gregory, London: Gaskell Press, 1998.

If you are supporting a person who needs to take prescription medicines, you may find the following booklet from the NHS useful – *Free Prescriptions: A Simple Guide* Ref.HC81(SG) available free from Department of Health, PO Box 777, London SE1.

If you want more advice about free prescriptions there is a free telephone helpline – 0800 9177711.

Points for practice
Help the person take any medicines and monitor their progress after they have seen the doctor.

3.6 Support for people who are incontinent

Incontinence is the term used describe an inability to retain urine or faeces. People who are incontinent have limited control of their bladder and/or bowels and may therefore leak urine or evacuate their bowels unpredictably and without any prior warning. This is relatively common among people with a learning disability and is likely to require both specific treatments and ongoing support from staff and carers.

Anyone can become incontinent for a variety of physical or psychological reasons. People with a learning disability may:

- not develop voluntary control of the bladder or bowels during childhood;
- experience increasing difficulty with bladder and/or bowel control as they get older;
- experience periodic bouts of incontinence.

In general, people with more severe and profound learning disability are more likely to experience incontinence.

Incontinence raises important issues for the health and welfare of the person concerned. From a purely practical point of view, absorbent pads and other aids are needed to minimise leakage. Good hygiene practices and regular cleansing are essential to keep the person comfortable and avoid infection. Just as important is the provision of support and advice to the person concerned so that they do not feel embarrassed and their incontinence does not restrict their lifestyle. Thirdly, it is essential not to assume that incontinence, when it occurs, is simply a consequence of the person's learning disability. Many people respond extremely well to support and treatment to promote continence.

Treatment for people who are incontinent

Anyone who is incontinent should be medically examined to identify any treatable conditions such as kidney or liver problems or urinary tract infections. These may cause incontinence or be a result of incontinence.

Faecal incontinence is more difficult to manage if the person is constipated or has diarrhoea. These conditions usually respond well to treatments such as improved diet, more exercise or medication. The GP can advise staff or carers on how to promote continence and, at the same time, help the person deal with the effects of incontinence.

Staff and carers can help by paying particular attention to skin care. At regular intervals, or more preferably after each urination or defecation, the person should be assisted to wash themselves and apply barrier creams to skin areas covered by the absorbent pads. A good fluid intake also helps to avoid constipation and inclusion of 400 ml of cranberry juice daily can reduce urinary infections.

Emotional and social factors

Effective and sensitive management of incontinence is essential to maintain the person's self-esteem and general sense of wellbeing. It will also reduce their dependence and enable them to participate in their usual work, leisure and recreational activities.

It is important to arrange for privacy and comfort when fitting continence pads and other aids. The person may also require assistance in choosing clothes which are comfortable, attractive and loose enough to disguise whatever continence aids are being used. A particular problem associated with faecal incontinence is unpleasant odour and it may be helpful to explore the use of personal deodorisers and 'air fresheners'.

It is important to avoid discussing a person's incontinence in public or anywhere which could give rise to embarrassment. People who experience incontinence should be encouraged to engage in a wide range of activities. Their incontinence should never be used to make fun of them or as a reason for excluding them from shared activities with other people.

4 Treatments requiring specialist medical services

Most treatments which require high levels of medical input involve admission to hospital and this can pose particular problems for people with a learning disability. As medical technology improves, there is a growing use of day-care to provide treatments which, in the past, were only available on an in-patient basis. Because day-care does not involve a person staying overnight in a strange place, it is often less stressful and less disruptive. It is, therefore, always worth asking if treatments can be carried out for a person with a learning disability on an out-patient or day care basis.

In this section we consider admission to hospital, support during a stay in hospital and what staff can do to help a person adjust after being discharged from hospital.

4.2 Admission to hospital

For anyone with a learning disability, the prospect of being taken into hospital is likely to raise a number of concerns. If this is their first admission for medical treatment, they may feel apprehensive about a whole range of issues. For example:

- What is it like in a hospital? People who have previously lived in a mental handicap hospital, may have inappropriate expectations about what life is like in a hospital.
- How long will I have to stay in hospital? Many people with a learning disability have difficulty with the concept of time, for example, when projecting forward, in terms of days or weeks.
- What will they do to me in hospital? Everyone who has been a hospital patient is familiar with the feeling of becoming a passive and helpless patient who must endure whatever kind of treatment the doctors decide is needed. These feelings are usually balanced by our confidence that the doctors and nurses are trying to make us better and our ability to ask questions and express our own views. In contrast, people with a learning disability may have inaccurate views about hospitals, ('most people who go into hospital die there') poor communication skills and little confidence in their ability to interact with other people. As a result, they are likely to feel particularly vulnerable, with little scope to influence hospital routines or find out about what lies in store for them.

- Will I come out again? For most of us, admission to hospital is associated with serious illness and treatments which could have serious side effects. One way of reassuring ourselves is to say that most people benefit from their treatment and come out of hospital feeling better. However, people with a learning disability may have developed negative ideas about what happens to people in hospitals. For example, they may remember a relative who died in hospital or they may have seen TV programmes which exaggerate the chances of dying in hospital. Additionally, many people with a learning disability have difficulty using the concept of risk (this operation is '99% successful') to understand their own situation.

In addition, there are the more ordinary, but no less important concerns about 'living' in a strange environment.

I won't know anyone there.

The people won't know me – perhaps they'll laugh at me or ignore me.

Where will I sleep?

Will it be noisy?

Will there be somewhere private to undress and bath?

Will I be able to watch my favourite programmes on the TV?

What will the food be like – will they make me eat things I don't like?

Can I wear my own clothes?

4.3 Support before and during admission to hospital

Once again, there are a number of things which staff can do to help a person with a learning disability who has to be admitted to hospital. First and foremost is the provision of information to address the questions and concerns described in the previous section.

You may need to consider the following:

- Who is the best person to explain the medical reasons for the admission to hospital? This involves having appropriate medical knowledge and the ability to communicate with the person concerned. You may decide that it will take two people to provide a really clear explanation – one to provide the medical information and another person, perhaps yourself, to explain it to the person with a learning disability.

- How can you provide information about what kinds of tests and treatment the person will have when they are in hospital? You may need to contact doctors or nursing staff prior to the admission and seek their help in developing a clear explanation. Staff may be concerned about discussing confidential information – in which case it may be helpful to involve a nurse from your local learning disability service.

- How can you find out whether the person you are working with has particular concerns about going into hospital and what can you do to reassure them? A preparatory visit might be useful, or you might wish to consider taking some photos or even a video film of the hospital.

- How you can help the hospital staff understand the person with a learning disability. Sometimes a written summary of their illness and their individual needs can help staff to respond appropriately.

Being admitted to hospital usually involves a number of different procedures and can take up to two hours. (An emergency admission, when the person's medical records are not easily available, often takes even longer.)

Registration

For planned admissions, the person will have received a letter or card telling them where to go when they arrive at the hospital. At this point you should ensure that the person's notes include a record of their learning disability, any associated special needs and the kinds of support they find helpful. This might include any of the following:

- Aids for communication, for example, signs, symbols etc.

- Additional medical problems, for example epilepsy.

- Unusual or erratic behaviours which might disturb anyone who is not prepared for them.

- Areas where they will need assistance, for example, using the toilet, getting dressed.

- Known risks for the person or to other people. For example, some people may be vulnerable to falls if left alone, while others may become aggressive or violent under certain circumstances.

- The names of the people who might need to be with the person during their stay in hospital. Make sure that the nursing staff recognise the need for these supporters to be available *outside the usual visiting hours.*

It is a good idea to have a summary of this information written or typed out ready for the nurse who arranges admissions to the hospital.

Preliminary examination

The patient may be asked to undress and they will be asked a number of questions about their medical condition and their current state of health. They will also be asked about medicines they are currently taking. If the person you are with takes prescription medicines, make sure they take them to the hospital and show them to the medical staff. (Remember that if you hand medicine over to the hospital staff, you may not get it back. When the person with a learning disability leaves the hospital, they will only provide a small amount of the medicine and he or she will need to visit the GP for another prescription.) Finally, a nurse will weigh the person being admitted and take their temperature and blood pressure. Usually, newly admitted patients are asked to dress in pyjamas or a nighty, (although they may have to wear a hospital gown if and when they have surgery). Make sure the person has their own night clothes with them. The smocks provided by most hospitals are uncomfortable and provide only limited cover for those of a modest disposition.

Allocation to a ward

A bed will be provided, probably in a large room or 'ward' with a number of other beds. Some of the other beds will be occupied and these other patients may be curious about the newcomer. Depending upon the time of day and the person's medical condition, they may be asked to get into bed or they may be able to stay up and use the day room.

The person you are with may find it difficult to settle into this strange environment. Here are some things you can do:

Unit 3

- Introduce yourself and the person with a learning disability to the other people on the ward and help them to make friends. Be direct and 'up-front' about the person's special needs, but be clear about their characteristics as a person, for example, you might encourage them to talk about their family or their hobbies or their favourite TV programmes. Don't forget that for many people in hospital, their own illness, and that of other people, is a major topic of conversation.

- Make sure that the nurse in charge of the ward knows about the person's learning disability and is aware of the special needs which you raised when the person registered.

- Make sure that the person with a learning disability knows about the practical aspects of being in hospital. For example:

  Where the toilets are

  When meals are served; how and when patients choose what they want to eat

  Where they can go to smoke (if this is permitted)

  How to summon help

  Where they can go to watch TV and how to select channels

  How to use the radio – most hospitals have radio earphones by each bed

  Visiting times

  Where the shops and cafes are and how to get to them.

- Make sure that the person has enough of their own possessions to feel secure and comfortable.

- Reassure the person about your availability (and the availability of their friends and relations) and tell them when you will visit next. If possible stay with them until the first meal has been served.

- Help the person maintain contact with the outside world by encouraging visits from other staff, friends and relations and arranging for the person with a learning disability to use a phone. Many hospitals do not permit the use of mobile phones because they interfere with medical equipment.

Emergency admissions

Of course, from time to time people enter hospital as an emergency admission, either following an accident, a sudden illness or a rapid and unexpected deterioration in a long standing (chronic) condition. In these circumstances, it will not be possible to undertake all the aspects of preparation described in the section above. However, it is important to explain as much as possible about what is happening and to make sure that someone who knows the person well accompanies them to the hospital. Whenever possible, follow the suggestions provided in relation to a planned hospital admission.

Activity 4

Make arrangements to visit your local hospital with one or two people with a learning disability. You might be able to do this when visiting another service user or a colleague who is in hospital. Alternatively, you might be able to incorporate the visit as part of a 'health awareness' project - make sure you take a letter from your manager which explains the purpose of your visit.

You won't be able to go everywhere, but you should be able to go into the main reception area and to the 'public areas' for use by visitors. Use the visit to find out what the people you are with know about hospitals and what kind of help they are likely to need if they ever have to be admitted to hospital.

Comment

Knowledge about hospitals varies a great deal; some people know a lot, often based on personal experience, while others know very little. Travel to and from hospital can be very difficult, and finding your way around hospitals presents problems for anyone who isn't able to read. Some people find that a big hospital building and the 'atmosphere' inside makes them feel uneasy. Older people with a learning disability may be reminded of their experiences of institutional care.

Points for practice
Accompany the person with a learning disability during admission to hospital and make sure the staff are aware of their special needs. Help the person settle into the hospital ward and to meet other patients.

4.4 Support during a stay in hospital

Apart from the discomfort and anxiety associated with being ill and receiving treatment, hospital can be distressing because of the way in which it:

disrupts everyday routines;

cuts people off from the outside world.

While there is little that can be done about the different routines that are imposed upon people in hospital, you can make a great deal of difference by keeping the person in touch with events going on at home and at work. Here are some suggestions:

- Encourage different people to visit; if possible arrange for at least one person to visit, even for a very brief period, each day.

- Talk to the person in hospital about their friends, family and what is happening in the places where they normally spend their time, for example, their home, their place of work, places they go for leisure.

- Take in recent photographs of people they know, pets, the garden etc., and use these to talk about what has been happening.

General anaesthetic

Major treatment procedures, such as operations, often cause anxiety. Some people do not want to know in detail what is involved, while others are curious and find the information reassuring. You may need to make a judgement about how much information the person with a learning disability can absorb and how far this will help them.

General anaesthetic involves loss of consciousness and, therefore, complete loss of control for the patient. Where the use of a general anaesthetic causes anxiety, it is probably related to this loss of control, together with the fear of 'not waking up again.' It is helpful to remind anyone having a general anaesthetic that this is a routine procedure, carried out by experienced and highly trained doctors. It doesn't involve any pain although, when waking up afterwards, some people feel sick for a short time.

And of course, the treatment itself may leave the patient feeling sore, bruised or with more intense pain which requires 'pain killers'. If the person with a learning disability is particularly worried about having a general anaesthetic, it is probably a good idea for someone they know well to be with them when the drugs are administered, until they become unconscious and then again after the treatment, when they 'wake-up'.

You will need to discuss this kind of arrangement in advance with the staff. Again, it is often helpful to find someone who has been through this experience to tell the person with a learning disability what to expect.

4.5 Discharge from hospital and continuing care

People who are discharged from hospital are seldom 'fit and free from illness'. In most cases they will require:

- an opportunity to rest and regain their strength;
- a time interval to find out whether the treatment has been successful;
- ongoing treatment in the form of medicines or visits to an out-patient clinic;
- follow-up treatment, such as physiotherapy, or occupational therapy.

The hospital should provide detailed information regarding what kind of care the person needs after discharge, and often this will be in the form of a printed sheet or booklet. The hospital should explain:

- how they expect the person to progress;
- when the person next needs to see a doctor or nurse;

- where they should go for checks on progress;
- what signs or symptoms would indicate complications and what action should be taken;
- who can be contacted for further advice.

As part of your role, you should make sure that this information is provided and that the person with a learning disability understands what they are expected to do. You may need to help the person make the arrangements for follow-up treatments or check-ups, including travel arrangements. They are also likely to need support in developing new routines which:

make allowances for physical limitations

highlight the times for taking medicines

fit in with visits for follow-up treatments.

If you are involved in supporting a person with a learning disability during a stay in hospital, you may find the following booklet useful: *Going Into Hospital* by Sheila Hollins, Angie Avis and Samantha Cheverton, London, Gaskell Press, 1998.

Points for practice
Help the person in hospital to maintain contact with what is happening 'outside' and when they are discharged, help them to establish routines which take account of any continuing health care needs.

5 Consent to treatment

It is reasonable to assume that doctors will only provide treatment which we want to receive and that we could, if we wished, refuse treatment. In English law patients have a considerable degree of protection, to the extent that even simple examination or giving an injection requires our consent. In practice, we give our consent by voluntarily going to the doctor's surgery or to the hospital and co-operating with the medical staff. It is the doctor's job to tell us about the treatment he or she is recommending so that we can make a judgement based upon good information, in other words we give informed consent.

It is helpful to think about consent as a three stage process:

having enough information to make a decision

being capable of making a decision

being able to communicate that decision to the doctor

Information about a medical treatment

On what basis is it possible to say that we know enough about a medical treatment to make a decision? Broadly speaking, there are four important questions to ask:

- what does the treatment involve?
- what is the treatment intended to achieve, in terms of the illness?
- what are the possible side effects and risks associated with the treatment?
- what will happen if you do not have the treatment? Are there any other treatments available?

For example, if the doctor suggests treating my hayfever with a course of injections, I want to know:

- how many injections I will need and where I will need to go to have the injection?

- what effect the doctor thinks the injections will have on my hayfever (clear it completely, or just make it a bit less uncomfortable?)
- are there any side effects like drowsiness or feeling sick?
- what is likely to happen if I don't have the injections – will the hayfever get worse, simply go away at the end of the summer, or could it be treated with a course of tablets instead?

Making a decision about medical treatment

In the above example, making a decision involves weighing up a number of bits of information in the light of my own feelings and personal preferences. For example, I really don't want the hassle of arranging appointments for injections, but, on the other hand, I'm pretty desperate to get something done about my hayfever. Perhaps I need to find out more about how the tablets work.

Communicating a decision about medical treatment

Very often patients in hospital feel as if they are swept along on a conveyor belt with doctors making decisions and simply telling the patient about what they have decided to do. Presumably, the doctors take the view that co-operation by the patient is a sign of consent. It is, therefore, important that someone creates an opportunity for communicating a decision about treatment. People who are confident and have good assertiveness skills may be able to do this for themselves, but most of us need some help.

Remember that doctors can only perform procedures which the patient has agreed to (except in life threatening emergencies). For example, if a doctor was carrying out an exploratory operation, it would be illegal to remove additional tissues or organs unless the patient had given consent or the removal was necessary to save the patient's life.

If the doctor responds to the patient's questions by providing information *and* the patient is able to understand and weigh up the pros and cons of the treatment on offer, *and* they are given an opportunity to communicate their decision, then they will have given *informed* consent.

5.2 Consent in the case of children

Not everyone is considered to have the mental capacity to consent to medical treatment. Children under the age of 16 years who can demonstrate sufficient understanding of a treatment may give consent on their own behalf, but for those without this level of understanding, consent must be given by their parents or those with parental responsibility. Refusal to have treatment by a child under the age of 16, even where he or she can demonstrate competence, can be overridden by a person with parental responsibility.

5.3 Can people with a learning disability give consent?

Some adults with a learning disability will not have the capacity to consent to treatment. However, there is no clear test of capacity, apart from judgements made by other people about:

- how well a person with a learning disability understands the proposed treatment;
- their ability to make a judgement;
- how well they are able to communicate that judgement.

Given the complexity of this 'test', it is inevitable that the 'capacity' of any single person will depend upon a whole range of circumstances. These include:

- the type of treatment under consideration, for example, it is easier to understand the implications of a tooth extraction compared to a hysterectomy;
- the amount of time available to explain and discuss the treatment;
- the level of support which is available;
- their previous experience of this treatment, either directly or from contact with another person.

Staff have a responsibility to ensure that everyone with a learning disability is given the opportunity to demonstrate their capacity to decide on medical treatments. This might involve:

- using pictures and diagrams to explain the treatment;
- using a cassette tape recording of the doctor's explanation – of course, it's important to ask the doctor before making a recording;
- talking to other people who have had the treatment;
- explaining and simplifying complicated language or medical terms;
- working through a series of 'what if ....' scenarios. For example: what if you had the operation, and afterwards you had a big scar on your tummy, how would you feel about that? Or, supposing you don't have the operation and you keep having these pains, how will you feel then?
- discussing the same points over a period of days (or maybe longer) to make sure the person has a settled view on the proposed treatment and they don't keep on changing their mind;
- encouraging the person with a learning disability to talk to at least two people, so that you can be sure their views were not influenced by one particular person.

Points for practice
Help the person with a learning disability to take an active role in making decisions about their treatment.

5.4 Treatment for people who cannot give consent

The law on consent to treatment was intended to protect vulnerable people from unscrupulous doctors. One unfortunate outcome is that a person who is not able to consent is likely to experience some difficulty in obtaining treatment, particularly if this involves surgery or other invasive procedures. Without consent, many treatment procedures could be considered illegal and the doctors concerned could be charged with a criminal or civil offence. It is important to remember that, as the law currently stands, if an adult is deemed unable to give consent, *no one can give consent on his or her behalf*. For this reason, you should refuse requests to give consent or sign a consent form for someone who cannot give consent to treatment themselves.

There are specific circumstances under which doctors can give treatment to people who are unable to give or withhold consent.

These are:

- emergency treatment which is designed to preserve life, assist recovery or ease suffering;
- treatment which is in the person's best interest and reflects a responsible body of medical opinion;
- where a High Court Judge has issued a 'declaration' that the treatment proposed would not be unlawful;
- treatment for a mental illness under the Mental Health Act.

This provides a limited solution to the problem of treatment without consent. However, there are considerable difficulties in applying these exceptions. For example, what constitutes an 'emergency' and what are the best interests of a person with a severe learning disability who is seriously ill but who might benefit from an unpleasant form of treatment which has numerous side effects? An additional problem is that many doctors are aware of the pitfalls in treating a person who cannot give consent, but they are not familiar with the precise circumstances in which they can act without consent. As a result the person with a learning disability who cannot give consent may have considerable difficulty in getting appropriate treatment.

5.5 Staff support for a person who cannot give consent

If you are sure that a person who needs medical treatment cannot give consent, it is important that you or your manager speaks to the person's GP at an early stage to explain the potential difficulties. The GP should be asked to consider whether the treatment might count as an emergency or whether it could be sanctioned as being in the person's best interests. In either case, the position should be set out by the GP in a letter to the hospital consultant responsible for treatment, explaining the pros and cons of the treatment for this patient and why it is regarded as necessary. He or she may also need to advise the hospital consultant about the legal position. The GP may wish to consult with learning disability psychiatrists or take advice from the local health authority. If this preparatory work is undertaken, the person with a learning disability should be able to receive the same treatment as any other patient.

Activity 5
Consider your best course of action in the following situations.

1. A middle-aged man with learning disabilities you work with enjoys gardening. He has been recommended a tetanus injection. You accompany him to the doctors, but when he sees the nurse prepare the injection he says very clearly that he's changed his mind and doesn't want to have the injection.

2. While you are with a young woman in the doctor's surgery, she mentions that she has a steady boyfriend and that she hopes to get married soon. The doctor asks what she is doing about 'birth control' and when the woman says 'nothing really' the doctor suggests she goes on the pill. The young woman looks confused, glances at you, but takes the prescription from the doctor.

3. You are with a man with severe learning disabilities who is told that he needs to have his wisdom tooth removed. During the consultation, he says very little, and just before you both leave, the dentist says casually to you, 'I'd like you to sign a consent form just to make sure that we do things by the book'.

Comment
In situation 1, you should support the man in his decision, so long as the doctor confirms that it is not an emergency. Later, you may decide to talk to him about: the treatment he is being offered; why it is necessary; what it involves; and what will happen if he doesn't have it. If he decides that he does wish to have the injection, he might benefit from some preparation.

In situation 2, the young woman is being asked to consent but it is not at all clear that she understands what she is consenting to. You should ask the doctor to explain what treatment he or she is proposing. If you think it would help, you could suggest that you speak to the woman about the proposed treatment over the next couple of days and come back to the doctor with her when she has had a chance to consider the idea of going on the pill.

In situation 3, you should explain to the dentist that you are not able to give consent on behalf of the man you are with. You have two options: if you think that the man could, with help, make an informed decision, you could suggest that he is given the time and opportunity to give consent to treatment; if you think that the man would not, even with help, be able to give informed consent, then you must make it clear that the decision lies with the dentist.

Points for practice

You cannot give consent for medical treatment to a person with a learning disability. Doctors are able to give treatment to a person who is unable to give consent in an emergency or if they can show that the treatment is clearly in the person's best interests. It is also possible for a doctor to provide treatment for a mental illness under the Mental Health Act.

6 Management of chronic and terminal illnesses

Like anyone else, people with a learning disability occasionally become ill over a long period of time. This is often referred to as 'chronic illness', and it includes conditions which can be effectively managed so that they have little impact on a person's lifestyle (such as asthma, diabetes and thyroid disorder) as well as more serious and debilitating conditions which require high levels of treatment and additional care.

6.2 Support for people with a chronic illness

The management of some chronic illness requires relatively simple treatments which can be delivered and monitored by the patient, with support from his or her family and carers, if necessary. For example, many people with diabetes take insulin by injection and only see their doctor for check-ups at intervals. In the case of a person with a learning disability staff may need to offer different kinds of help:

- ensuring that the treatment (medicines, physiotherapy etc) is taken as prescribed;
- helping the person monitor their condition and to seek medical advice in the event of any unexpected changes;
- encouraging the person to lead a full and active life, even though they have chronic illness.

Other types of chronic illness involve higher levels of medical input. This is likely to have a much greater impact on a person's quality of life and in some cases ongoing distress and discomfort, arising either from the condition itself or as a result of some of the treatment procedures. Examples of such conditions are rheumatoid arthritis, and, more rarely, leukaemia. The care of people with these, or similar, conditions is likely to be much more focussed on the provision of treatment to alleviate the symptoms of illness. Ordinary activities, such as going shopping, having a night out at the pub or going on a day-trip are likely to be planned around the treatment and fitted in as and when the person feels able to participate. Staff will need to think about activities which are both feasible and enjoyable for the person with the chronic illness and carefully plan how these can be made available to them.

6.3 Terminal illness

This is the term used to describe any illness which does not respond to treatment and eventually 'terminates' in death (see Unit 1). It is important to bear in mind that sooner or later many of us will die from some kind of 'terminal illness' and that as other causes of death (such as accidents or short term 'acute' infection) are brought under control, it is more likely that people will die from some sort of longer term 'terminal' illness. The most common causes of death among older people are:

Cardiovascular disease;
Cancer;
Chronic obstructive pulmonary disease, such as thrombosis;
Pneumonia;
Diabetes mellitus;
Accidents.

Different terminal illnesses are associated with different symptoms and require different kinds of treatment. Some illnesses are associated with a great deal of discomfort and require high levels of medical input simply to alleviate pain and distress. Others can be managed in a less intrusive way. One of the most significant differences is the time scale during which the illness progresses. Some illnesses usually result in death after a few day or weeks, while others progress gradually, perhaps in response to treatment, and only result in death after many months or even years.

Similarly, individual people respond differently to terminal illness, both physically and psychologically; people suffering from the same illness may appear to experience different levels of pain or discomfort, have their lifestyle affected to a greater or lesser extent and appear more or less distressed by the progress of the illness. When supporting people with a terminal illness, it is important to respond to their needs, rather than to make judgements about their personal strengths or frailties.

There are a number of ways in which staff can help:

- Find out about the illness and how it progresses.
- Be prepared for the person's health and sense of well-being to vary from day to day.

- Make sure you know what treatment is being used and where and when it is provided; consider whether you have a role in the provision of treatment.
- Make sure you know the best ways of making the person comfortable and how to reduce pain and physical discomfort.
- Consider how you can provide interest and variety in the person's life and what you can do to maintain this as their physical condition changes.

Activity 6
Think of one person you know well, or have worked with in the past, who has a chronic or terminal illness. Make a list of the things which you and other members of staff have done:

a) to help with any treatment;

b) to maintain his/her quality of life as the illness progressed.

Comments
Help with treatment can include things like reminding someone to take their medicine; helping the person arrange transport to and from the place where treatment is provided; giving the person support and encouragement if they have to undertake treatment which is painful or uncomfortable.

For 'maintaining quality of life' you should include any examples of helping the person to continue with interests and activities which are made more difficult by the illness or by the treatment. You might also have included things you have done to keep the person comfortable and minimise discomfort.

Points for practice
For people who have long term or terminal illnesses you can help to minimise discomfort and provide variety and interest in their day to day lives.

Unit 3

7 Bereavement and preparation for death

People with a learning disability will sooner or later encounter death, either because someone they know – a relative, friend or neighbour – dies or because they themselves are seriously ill and likely to die. In either case, they will need support, particularly from their family and/or members of staff. The nature of the support provided will need to reflect the person's level of understanding about what happens when someone dies.

The information and advice in the final sections of this unit are based upon the three BILD publications:

Understanding Death and Dying:

- *Your Feelings*
- *A Guide for Families and Friends*
- *Guide for Carers and other Professionals*

by Fiona Cathcart, available from Plymbridge Distributors, price £10. Tel: 01752 202301

and

When Dad Died
When Mum Died

by Sheila Hollins and Lester Sireling, available from the Royal College of Psychiatrists, price £10 each. Tel: 020 7235 2351.

7.2 What happens when someone dies?

While there are many different ideas about the afterlife and what happens to a person's soul or spirit when they die, there are aspects of death which are universally recognised:

- Dead people are separated from the living – we cannot communicate with them.
- After death people do not move.
- After death, all parts of a person's body stop working.
- People who are dead cannot see or hear; think or feel.
- Death is permanent – once a person is dead, they can never come back to life.
- Death happens to everyone, sooner or later.

People with a learning disability vary in the extent to which they understand all these aspects of death. As a result, they may not fully understand the implications of death for themselves or for other people. For example, if someone does not understand that death is a permanent state, or that death happens to everyone sooner or later, they may find it difficult to adjust when an older relative, such as their mother or father, dies.

7.3 Teaching people about death

Perhaps the worst possible time to learn about death is when the person concerned, or someone they love, is dying. Illness makes any kind of learning and adjustment difficult, while the emotional distress of being 'left' by someone who dies is also likely to inhibit new learning. It is much easier if people with a learning disability are helped to find out about death, as a normal and fairly ordinary event, in the course of their everyday lives. For example, the death of a pet or a TV character might provide the starting point for a conversation during which you can explore how much the person understands about what happens when someone dies.

Use the six items set out above as a framework and make a note of any areas where the person seems unsure or confused. When another opportunity to talk about death comes up, try to steer the conversation around to that particular topic. Try to build up the person's understanding of death gradually and make as much use as you can of their own experience. Avoid using terms which might be misunderstood, for example, saying someone has 'gone to heaven' might suggest that, rather than dying, they have moved away and 'deserted' the person with a learning disability.

Points for practice

Use everyday experiences as opportunities to help people with a learning disability understand what happens when someone dies.

7.4 Bereavement

Everyone responds to the death of someone they know well in different ways. This partly reflects our personality, and partly our upbringing and what we have learned about grieving. People from different cultures often express their grief in different ways.

Unit 3

People with a learning disability may show their grief in a 'traditional' way, for example, by crying or becoming withdrawn. Alternatively, they may show grief in unusual and unpredictable ways. For example they might:

- become clingy and not want to be left alone;
- avoid going out;
- become incontinent;
- deliberately injure themselves;
- destroy property;
- become restless;
- experience aches and pains;
- have disturbed sleep;
- experience changes in appetite;
- become apathetic or listless;
- become susceptible to minor illnesses;
- appear clumsy and accident prone.

Some people show very few outward signs of grief, and yet inwardly feel just as upset as anyone else. It is important that you are able to recognise all these behaviours as symptoms of grief and offer support and understanding. In particular, you can help by:

- talking to the person with a learning disability about what has happened;

- in the case of a family member, asking them if they would like to view the body and making the arrangements. (You will need to make sure that this does not conflict with the family's cultural practices);

- helping them to attend the funeral – they may be able to take part, for example, by taking flowers;

- talking with them about the person who died – they might like to make a book of photographs or other mementos;

- helping them to talk to other people and participate in the mourning rituals appropriate to their community and culture.

Unit 3

Activity 7

Consider how you could help the following people come to terms with death and dying:

1. John's pet budgerigar died about six weeks ago. One of the temporary staff threw the dead bird out with the rubbish 'so as not to upset the residents' while John was at college. John is still very distressed and every morning he looks in the empty cage as if he expects to see 'Bertie the budgie'.

2. Pat's Auntie Noreen visited him every week until she died suddenly about two weeks ago. Pat was told that she had 'passed away' and wouldn't be coming back. The funeral took place in Ireland and Pat wasn't invited. Pat still asks when Auntie Noreen will be coming to see him.

3. Joshua has become very withdrawn and sullen recently. He seems to have lost his appetite and he has started to have nightmares. Nobody seems to know what's wrong and the doctor said that physically he is fine, although he seems a little depressed. One of Joshua's friends said he was sad because one of the characters in Joshua's favourite TV 'soap' had been murdered.

Comment

All three of these situations provide an opportunity to extend the person's understanding of death and dying as well as helping them to come to terms with specific events.

You could help John by explaining exactly what happened to Bertie. This might be a good opportunity to help John understand that death is permanent. If he decides to have another budgie, try to make sure that it is not confused with Bertie, for example, you might suggest a different colour and different name.

You could help Pat by explaining what happened to his auntie and, if possible, arranging a visit to the place where she was buried/cremated. If this is not possible, pictures of the church or crematorium might help you to describe what happens after death. Pat might feel better if he has some pictures of his auntie and the opportunity to talk to you and other people about her.

If Joshua doesn't fully understand the difference between 'death' on the TV and death in real life, it is quite reasonable for him to show signs of grief when a character he knows well gets murdered. Don't assume that Joshua's isn't real – he is likely to need the same support as anyone else who is grieving over a death. As Joshua gets over his grief, you might decide to help him understand that the actor didn't actually die, although for real people death is permanent.

Points for practice
Be aware of the different ways in which people with a learning disability may respond to the death of a loved one and be prepared to help them express their grief in ways which are appropriate to their religion and culture.

7.6 Preparation for death

Death is one of the most intensely personal and sensitive events. In most western countries dying is a private affair and one which most people prefer not to talk about. As a result, most people have little idea about what it is like to die or how to prepare themselves for death. As a consequence, most of us are poorly prepared to help others such as those with a learning disability.

There are three areas in which preparation before death may be helpful.

1. Practical arrangements. When they know that they are going to die, many people want to 'put their affairs in order'. This might involve any of the following:

    making a will
    paying outstanding bills
    making arrangements for the care of pets
    getting rid of possessions which are no longer needed
    destroying private documents or giving them to a trusted friend or relation
    discussing funeral arrangements

2. Saying goodbye. Very often people who are dying want to see friends and family 'before they go'. Sometimes this is an

opportunity to remember good times or to celebrate longstanding relationships. For some people it is an opportunity to put the record straight or to apologise for past wrongs. During these meetings people need time to be together and to relax with each other. Often, the dying person will want repeated opportunities to 'say goodbye' to the same person, right up until they finally die.

3. Personal thoughts and feelings. Dying people experience a variety of different emotions ranging from fear to remorse to anger. With time, and sometimes help from family friends or an experienced counsellor, many people become more peaceful and accepting of death. As they move closer to death, many people find that their spiritual life becomes more important and some will want religious guidance and support.

Anyone with a learning disability who is dying will need support in each of these areas. Staff should consider:

- What can be done to help the person make the necessary practical arrangements?
- Do they need help to spend time with their family and friends?
- Are they in need of someone to offer spiritual guidance, for example, a priest or counsellor?

8 Concluding comments

This unit has covered a number of topics which will help you provide support for people with a learning disability who need treatment. Very often treatment can be provided at the doctor's surgery or at an out-patient clinic. Even for quite minor forms of treatment, many people with a learning disability will benefit from preparation and support. It is always a good idea to find out if they want someone to go with them when they need treatment.

More complex forms of treatment are likely to require admission to hospital. This can be a confusing and frightening experience and most people with a learning disability will benefit from support before, during and after their stay in hospital.

Any form of treatment must be carried out with the consent of the patient and staff have an important role to play in helping the people they work with give informed consent. If a person cannot give consent himself or herself, then the doctors who give the treatment must decide whether treatment is required as an emergency procedure or if it is clearly in the person's best interest.

Some people will experience long term or 'chronic' conditions which require ongoing treatment and have major consequences for the person's lifestyle. Some conditions are 'progressive' and eventually cause death. People with a learning disability will need extensive help to respond in a positive way to either chronic or terminal illness. Staff can help people with a learning disability to prepare for death and bereavement and, when death is inevitable, they should help people make appropriate arrangements.

Unit 3

References

Hollins, S., Avis, A. and Cheverton, S. (1998) *Going Into Hospital,* London: Gaskell Press

Hollins, S., Bernal, J. and Gregory, M. (1998) *Going to Outpatient's,* London: Gaskell Press

Hollins, S. and Sireling, L. (1989) *When Dad Died,* London: Gaskell Press

Hollins, S. and Sireling, L. (1989) *When Mum Died,* London: Gaskell Press

These and other books in the Books Beyond Words series are available from the Royal College of Psychiatrists, 17 Belgrave Square, London SW1X 8PG, Tel 020 7235 2351.

Cathcart, F. (1994)
Understanding Death and Dying:
- *Your Feelings;*
- *A Guide for Families and Friends*
- *Guide for Carers and other Professionals*

These BILD books are available from Plymbridge Distributors Tel: 01752 202301

Free prescriptions: A Simple Guide, Ref.HC81(SG) available free from Department of Health, PO Box 777, London SE1

Advice about free prescriptions - free Telephone Helpline – 0800 9177711

Unit 3

Summary of points for practice

1. Most people with a learning disability will benefit from preparation before they receive minor medical treatments such as an injection.
2. Provide support during minor treatments by explaining what is happening and helping the doctors and nurses to relate positively to the person with a learning disability.
3. Help the person take any medicines and monitor their progress after they have seen the doctor.
4. Accompany the person with a learning disability during admission to hospital and make sure the staff are aware of their special needs. Help the person settle into the hospital ward and to meet other patients.
5. Help the person in hospital to maintain contact with what is happening 'outside' and when they are discharged, help them to establish routines which take account of any continuing health care.
6. Help the person with a learning disability to take an active role in making decisions about their treatment.
7. You cannot give consent for medical treatment to a person with a learning disability. Doctors are able to give treatment to a person who is unable to give consent in an emergency or if they can show that the treatment is clearly in the person's best interests. It is also possible for a doctor to provide treatment for a mental illness under the Mental Health Act.
8. For people who have long term or terminal illnesses you can help to minimise discomfort and provide variety and interest in their day to day lives.
9. Use everyday experiences as opportunities to help people with a learning disability understand what happens when someone dies.
10. Be aware of the different ways in which people with a learning disability may respond to the death of a loved one and be prepared to help them express their grief in ways which are appropriate to their religion and culture.